At Night

Written by Emma MacDonald

Collins

moths near a roof

barn owls

moths near a roof

barn owls

big ears

a long tail

big ears

a long tail

near a log

down in the soil

11

near a log

down in the soil

 Review: After reading

Use your assessment from hearing the children read to choose any GPCs, words or tricky words that need additional practice.

Read 1: Decoding

- Use grapheme cards to make any words you need to practise. Model reading those words, using teacher-led blending.
- Ask the children to follow as you read the whole book, demonstrating fluency and prosody.

Read 2: Vocabulary

- Look back through the book and discuss the pictures. Encourage the children to talk about details that stand out for them. Use a dialogic talk model to expand on their ideas and recast them in full sentences as naturally as possible.
- Work together to expand vocabulary by naming objects in the pictures that children do not know.
- On page 2 discuss the meaning of **near**. Ask: What is the owl near? What are the moths near? (*the roof*) Ask the children to point to things that are near to where they are sitting.

Read 3: Comprehension

- Talk about animals that come out at night. Encourage the children to describe any they have seen or read about in books. Ask: What were they like? Where were they?
- Ask the children which of the animals are **down in the soil**? Encourage them to look through the pages to find the answer. (*the badger, page 11*)
- Turn to pages 14 and 15. Encourage the children to describe each of the creatures. Prompt with questions, such as: Where are the moths? (*near a roof*) Can you describe the rabbit's ears? (*big*)